INTELLIGENT LEARNING SYSTEMS ADAPTIVE AND GAME BASED

INTELLIGENT LEARNING SYSTEMS ADAPTIVE AND GAME BASED

BY

MIA WALKER
AUTON GILL

KNOWLEDGE BAKERS

KNOWLEDGE BAKERS

ISBN: 9789390013418 (HB)

Published by : **Knowledge Bakers**
Pune, India
Email: knowledgebakers2019@gmail.com

Printed at : : **Replika Press Pvt Ltd**

PREFACE

With regard to Gardener's multiple intelligence theory, the introduction of all intelligences in the education system is of great advantage to the learners and society at large. As explained by Gardener, "initial ways of intelligence testing are not competent due to their biases to only one type of intelligence". Introduction of all intelligences in the education systems will enable individuals get the understanding that everyone has got a mind of their own. Through the introduction of the various intelligences in schools, parent and the teachers will be in a position to understand an individual weak points and strengths through determining a preferred learning method. According to Gardener, he believes that the development of morality can be achieved through learning a single intelligence. 'The use of various intelligences would enable the students to grow morals prohibited through various intelligences like the music intelligence'. Another benefit of the multiple intelligence, education system is that it enables the students not get evaluated according to the IQ level. Gardener has referred to this as a shallow idea. Therefore, students will have various disciplines to be examined, maybe through observations, student's portfolio work and other ways.

Intelligent adaptive learning is a new class of education technology that captures every decision a student makes and adjusts the student's learning path both within lessons and between lessons, thereby providing millions of individualized learning paths, each tailored to a student's unique needs in real time. Adaptive learning systems (often called adaptive learning environments) aim at supporting learners in acquiring knowledge and skills in a particular learning domain. The goal is to enhance the individual learning process with respect to speed, accuracy, quality and quantity of learning.

It provides an introduction to the concept of game-based and adaptive learning, including their benefits and potential applications in various settings. It explores the role of games in education and how they can be used to engage students and improve learning outcomes. It covers topics such as educational game design principles, types of games used in education, and examples of successful implementations. It focuses on the use of simulations in learning, including their advantages and limitations and discusses various types of simulations, such as virtual simulations, role-playing simulations, and interactive simulations, and their applications in different domains. It covers the concept of gamification, which involves incorporating game elements and mechanics into non-game contexts to motivate and engage learners and explores the use of virtual worlds in learning, including their potential benefits and challenges. It provides examples of how faculty members have incorporated game-based and adaptive learning strategies into their teaching practices. It includes case studies, examples of successful implementations, and tips for getting started with game-based and adaptive learning. This book will be an indispensable source of information for scientists, educators, engineers, and technical staff active in all fields of learning.

We are grateful to all those persons as well as various books, manuals, periodicals, magazines, journals etc. that helped in the preparation of this book. In spite of the best efforts, it is possible that some errors may have occurred into the compilation and editing of the book. Further queries, constructive suggestions and criticisms for the improvement of the book are always welcomed and shall be thankfully acknowledged.

Mia Walker
Auton Gill

CONTENTS

Introduction

This book is designed to accompany a graduate-level instructional design course: ***Game-Based and Adaptive Learning*** but could also be used for undergraduate teacher education or instructional design courses.

The original texts and material for this book came from the development of a course for Brandeis University as part of their MS in Learner Experience Design program. This material can be used to teach pre-service teachers, in-service teachers, and instructional designers about game-based and adaptive learning. Assessments used in the actual Game-based and Adaptive Learning course are included in the final chapter and serve as recommendations for assessments of the learning outcomes. The material in this book pairs well with Using Game-Based Learning Online – A Cookbook of Recipes by The EGG.

The Faculty Showcase materials were developed by dedicated faculty during the course of a year-long game development workshop in which faculty were introduced to GBL, developed game prototypes, played a variety of games, and finally playtested their designs. The work they continue to do in the area of GBL is part of the inspiration for this book. If you would like to contribute your own case study, please contact me at carrie.miller@mnsu.edu for consideration.

Suggested Learning Outcomes

Course Level and Module Level Outcones

CARRIE LEWIS MILLER

Course Outcomes:

1. Describe the learner traits and characteristics of those most positively impacted by game-based and adaptive learning
2. Identify and analyze organizational opportunities for the adoption of game-based or adaptive learning to achieve instructional outcomes
3. Compare adaptive learning, gamification, games, or simulations as used in learning and apply each to appropriate learning scenarios
4. Examine technology tools to create adaptive or game-based learning solutions
5. Design appropriate adaptive learning solution and implementation strategy for a global organization and its learning technology ecosystem
6. Develop a storyboard, prototype, or detailed design document of an original adaptive or game-based learning solution
7. Evaluate commercially available adaptive and game-based learning solutions for adaptability into your own organization

Module Level Outcomes:

1. Define Game-Based Learning
2. Identify traits common to gamers
3. Distinguish between Games, Gamification, Simulations, Virtual

Worlds, and Adaptive Learning
4. Categorize elements of games in order to apply those elements to educational gaming
5. Explain Adaptive Learning
6. Recommend Adaptive Learning Solutions for your own organizational context
7. Identify tools for use to create adaptive learning experiences
8. Create a -Mini Adaptive Learning Experience
9. Plan multiple methods of creating adaptive learning experiences
10. Summarize the current availability of serious games and digital games for educational purposes
11. Select 2-3 digital games for potential use in your own organizational context
12. Describe the use of non-digital games in educational or training contexts
13. Create a non-digital game solution to an educational or training problem
14. Debate the impact of commercial games on education and training
15. Evaluate commercially available games for use in educational contexts
16. Distinguish between high-fidelity and digital simulations
17. Describe opportunities to integrate simulations into educational contexts
18. Debate the value of gamification strategies in learning
19. Prepare an outline for a gamification strategy for an instructional module
20. Summarize the benefits and challenges of implementing a badging system
21. Identify badging platforms
22. Create 3-4 badges for a learning experience that the learners are familiar with
23. Define the term virtual worlds
24. Identify examples of virtual world platforms

25. Assess the digital safety concerns of implementing learning environments in virtual worlds
26. Define Virtual Reality
27. Identify options for integrating VR into learning environments
28. Differentiate between VR and AR
29. Explore AR apps for use in education

PART I

CHAPTER 1 - OVERVIEW OF THE GAME-BASED AND ADAPTIVE LEARNING

1. Game-Based Learning

Game-Based Learning

Learning Objectives

- Define Game-Based Learning
- Distinguish between Games, Gamification, Simulations, Virtual Worlds, and Adaptive Learning

Game-based learning (GBL)is an active learning strategy that is an intersection between game elements and the learning environment, using strategies typically reserved for games to encourage and enhance learning, practice, and assessment. Game-based learning relies on defined learning outcomes and often uses a cycle of failure, reflection, and repetition to provide safe yet meaningful learning experiences for students. Over the past decade, game-based learning has grown tremendously in the classroom. If you considered using digital games to help students learn a few decades ago, people would have thought of you as unconventional and a maverick. Today, game-based learning is more widely known and used by many teachers who have their students play games at least weekly (Takeuchi & Vaala, 2014). GBL is not restricted to digital games but encompasses a wide variety of strategies that include board games, gamification, simulations, and adaptive learning. Figure 1 shows the differences between the various strategies.

	Game-based Learning	Gamification	Simulations
Brief Definition	A type of gameplay that has defined learning outcomes	The application of game elements to non-game activities or contexts	A controlled environment is as realistic as possible where learners can practice behaviors free of risk
Major points	Serious games Games Gamification	Motivation Rewards	Impact of decisions Practice
Examples	Win the White House	Lose It	Nursing Gap

Figure 1. Comparison of GBL, gamification, simulations, and adaptive learning.

Game-based learning involves designing learning activities so that game principles and characteristics are embedded within the learning activities themselves. It can also involve transforming commercially available games into a learning experience. Research shows that both gamification and game-based learning have the potential to promote student engagement and motivation in learning in a variety of disciplines (Pesare et al., 2016). GBL uses competitive exercises, either pitting the students against each other or getting them to challenge themselves to motivate them to learn better.

Storytelling is essential in games and game-based learning and it is the story that provides the context for gameplay. When using a GBL strategy, it is important for instructors to determine what story they will tell or what story the game will tell, in order to encourage students to connect game-play with the curriculum.

Games often have a fantasy element that engages players in a learning activity through a storyline. In order to create a truly educational game, the instructor needs to make sure that learning or practicing the material is essential to successfully completing the game. Teachers need to work out how to give students points for accomplishing certain goals in a lesson plan and decide on rewards for the winners. Students should receive immediate feedback on their performance from either the game or the instructor along with suggestions on how to improve.

Integration of learning with gaming makes subjects more fun. It can also motivate students to learn, which can have an impact on student engagement. GBL allows students to drill and practice certain skills, knowledge, or behavior by immersing them in a virtual environment (Jan & Gaydos, 2016). Games can promote logical and critical thinking and the development of social skills, language abilities, communication skills, and creative and problem-solving capabilities (McFarlane et al., 2002). Game-based learning supports pedagogical principles such as:

- Individualization: The level of the game is tailored on the basis of the player's abilities.
- Feedback: Immediate and contextualized feedback is supplied during the game session.
- Active learning: The game engages the player in active discovery.
- Motivation: The players are engaged in pursuing a goal.
- Social: The game is often multiplayer or social.
- Scaffolding: Players are gradually challenged because they cannot move freely among the game levels.
- Transfer: The game fosters the ability to transfer learning from the game context to a real context.
- Assessment: The player can assess the acquired knowledge or skill with other players (Pesare et al., 2016, p. 4).

Question for Discussion

1. What does game-based learning mean to you?
2. What opportunities for using game-based

learning do you see in your own organization?

3. What challenges might you encounter when implementing game-based learning?

References

Jan, M., & Gaydos, M. (2016). What is game-based learning? Past, present, and future. Educational Technology, 56(3), 6-11.

McFarlane, A., Sparrowhawk, A., & Heald, Y. (2002). *Report on the educational use of games: Teachers evaluating educational multimedia.* Cambridge.

Pesare, E., Roselli, T., & Corriero, N. (2016). Game-based learning and gamification to promote engagement and motivation in medical learning contexts. *Smart Learn. Environ*, 3(5). https://doi.org/10.1186/s40561-016-0028-0

Takeuchi, L. M., & Vaala, S. (2014). *Level up learning: A national survey on teaching with digital games.* New York: The Joan Ganz Cooney Center at Sesame Workshop.

Recommended Supplementary Material

- Plass, J. L., Homer, B. D., & Kinzer, C. K. (2015). Foundations of game-based learning. Educational Psychologist, 50(4), 258-283. https://doi.org/10.1080/00461520.2015.1122533
- Spires, H. A. (2015). Digital Game-Based

learning. *Journal of Adolescent & Adult Literacy*, 59(2), 125-130. http://doi.org/10.1002/jaal.424

- Use the Four Gamer Types to Help Your Students Collaborate – from Douglas Kiang on Edudemic

- *A TED element has been excluded from this version of the text. You can view it online here: https://mlpp.pressbooks.pub/gamebasedlearning/?p=5*

- *Warning – Contains Simulated Video Game Violence*
- https://youtube.com/watch?v=1JqR3GVqib4%3Flist%3DELLdMMObVx91g
- Using Game-based Learning Online – A Cookbook of Recipes

2. Who are Gamers?

Learning Objectives

- Identify traits common to gamers

A "Gamer" is a term that refers to anyone who routinely plays games. While it is generally used in reference to video games, it can also mean board games, card games, or role-playing games. Whether it is a hobby or a profession, gamers play to interact, collaborate, socialize, and win games.

Stereotypically, we think of gamers as introverted teenagers or children but actually, the average age of gamers is currently 35-44 years of age. In fact, 9% of gamers are over the age of 55! Almost half (41%) of gamers are female (2020 Essential Facts About the Video Game Industry, 2021). Not all people who play games regularly consider themselves "gamers." In fact, most people who play games do not identify themselves by that term. Culturally, the term "gamer" can have somewhat negative connotations, often referring to someone who chooses to play video games over any other type of activity.

Whether or not a player chooses to identify as a "gamer," most people who play games can be placed into a category on a gamer characteristic taxonomy. Bartle's is the most well-known gamer taxonomy, using a personality inventory matrix to place gamers into one of four categories, as seen in Figure 2.

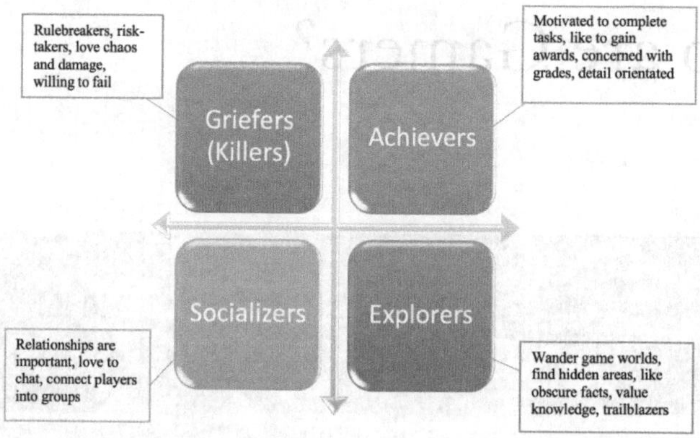

Figure 2. Four types of gamers according to Bartle's Taxonomy.

However, Bartle's taxonomies were designed to apply only to a specific type of gamer, those that play Massively Multiplayer Online Role-Playing Games (MMORPG). Further studies of gamers and their gaming habits have shown that a player may show tendencies towards one category while playing a certain game, then show tendencies of a different category when playing a different game. In addition, players can often drift between categories, leading some to be on the border of two (e.g., Achiever-Killer or Socializer-Achiever).

Gamers spend an average of 6.5 hours per week playing games. The range of gameplay can fall from "newbie" or "noob" and "casual" to "hardcore." The category with which a player self-identifies tends to depend on their reason for gameplay, the time spent on gameplay, and the level of competition involved.

Gamers have their own vocabulary (online glossary) and are accustomed to common game mechanics. Leaderboards, leveling up, farming, guilds or clans, avatars, customization, XP, and training levels are all common elements in gaming.

There are professional gamers and gaming competitions. Wil Wheaton is probably one of the more well-known gamers who has competed in Dungeons & Dragons contests and who hosts his own game instruction TV show, Tabletop. Gamers often screencast themselves during gameplay and stream their videos live on sites such as Twitch.

Question for Discussion

1. Take the Bartle Test of Gamer DNA. In your discussion post, share your results with us. Does this fit your gameplay style? Why or why not? If you don't consider yourself a "gamer," did your results surprise you? What traits would you identify with someone who plays games?

References

2020 Essential Facts About the Video Game Industry. (2021). *Entertainment Software Association.* https://www.theesa.com/wp-content/uploads/2020/07/Final-Edited-2020-ESA_Essential_facts.pdf

Kiang, D. (2014, January 21). *Use the four gamer types to help your students collaborate.* Edtechteacher. https://edtechteacher.org/use-the-four-gamer-types-to-help-your-students-collaborate-from-douglas-kiang-on-edudemic/

3. What makes a game a game?

Learning Objectives

- Categorize elements of games in order to apply those elements to educational gaming

What is a game? We can probably think of many types of games, but in general, a game is an activity with a specific goal and a defined set of rules that is usually completed for the amusement of the players.

Any game has one or more game elements such as rules, goals, rewards, challenges, competition, or chance. Games take many forms such as digital, board, card, physical, computer, hand-held, mobile, sports, and paper. Games can be for fun, for pleasure, for education, or for competition.

One of the fundamental elements of any game is providing a common experience to any player. This is not to say that all players will have the same experience or the same outcomes, but that within the confines of the game, each player will have at least some sort of shared experience and vocabulary. All games must also allow for the individual freedom of the player within the boundaries set up by the rules of the game.

Games generally have a system of artificial conflict built into the rules or elements of the game. This may be between players, between the player and the computer, or between the player and his/herself. Conflict in this sense doesn't necessarily mean fighting or direction competition. It means challenges and obstacles that must be overcome to beat the game.

Almost any game also has a story. It may be rescuing a princess, finding your way out of a swamp, collecting jacks, or creating a successful farm, but a story is there that lives in the background of the game and drives the gameplay forward.

A game also has a resolution. At some point, there is an end to the game, presumably because someone or a group of someones have "won" the game. How a player wins depends entirely on the goal of the game. Some games may not have clear winners at the end of the game. Tic Tac Toe is one such game where chance or strategy can often dictate a draw where neither player "wins" the game.

Games can be social or collaborative in nature or they can be designed for single players. Most commercial digital games currently available are single-player games that offer the option to have "co-op" (co-operative) play online. While often we think of this type of gaming behavior as isolationist, preliminary studies would seem to suggest that a good deal of socialization occurs in the online gaming environment and players tend to build their own social networks complete with social rules and norms.

Think of a game you play often. What are the game elements? What are the game mechanics? What freedom do you have as a player within the game? What is the story of the game?

Question for Discussion

1. If you don't currently play a game or simulation, do a google search. Choose a game or simulation that you can play for the duration of the class. You

don't have to spend a ton of time on it, you just need to play it consistently at least once a week. This can be a video game, board game, real or digital simulation, app, educational game, a game you play with your kids – in short, anything. Identify the game you have chosen to play. Why did you select that game? Is it a game, simulation, virtual world, or an adaptive learning experience?

4. Adaptive Learning

Learning Objectives

- Explain Adaptive Learning
- Recommend Adaptive Learning Solutions for your own organizational context
- Identify tools for use to create adaptive learning experiences
- Create a -Mini Adaptive Learning Experience
- Plan multiple methods of creating adaptive learning experiences

Adaptive learning is an interactive method that generally harnesses the logic of computers to create individualized pathways for student learning. The adaptive learning environment guides a learner through the content based on responses to a series of knowledge checks, increasing or decreasing the complexity of the content as indicated by the learner responses.

Commercial adaptive learning solutions exist, and companies, such as Dreambox and Knewton, provide adaptive learning platforms for instructors to use. Many textbook publishers, such as Pearson and McGraw-Hill, have created adaptive learning software packages as online tools or "labs" for students to explore and practice. Most learning management systems can be utilized to create adaptive learning experiences on a smaller scale.

Adaptive learning is often a fundamental component of gameplay.

For those who have played commercial video games, you may have experienced the difficulty or complexity of the game increasing as you make "correct" choices in your character's actions. Some games will introduce varying scenarios based on a particular player's choices while playing the game, increasing the personalization and replayability of the game.

It is important to distinguish between game-based and adaptive learning, however. While game-based learning may contain adaptive learning elements, adaptive learning may not always contain game mechanics in its design.

Traditionally, adaptive learning by definition includes the use of computers. I would argue that because the fundamental component of adaptive learning is the idea of personalized learning pathways, based on user responses or choices, adaptive learning experiences can be built into a learning experience without the need for technology.

At the heart of adaptive learning is the learning pathway. Learning pathways are built using branching logic, also known as conditional branching. Most often used in reference to online surveys, branching logic maps out the possible response paths a user can choose when interacting with an online experience. For all intents and purposes, branching logic is a map to all possible avenues a student can take to approach a learning experience. The example below in Figure 3 might be a possible adaptive learning pathway to a lesson on the wives of Henry VIII of England. Each correctly answered question or completed task propels the learner further through the content. For each incorrect answer, feedback and opportunities for review are provided. Rather than just questions, content information could be provided at each critical junction (represented by the squares). Possible responses are noted in the diamond shapes. Formative feedback is represented in the ovals with review information in the cylinder.

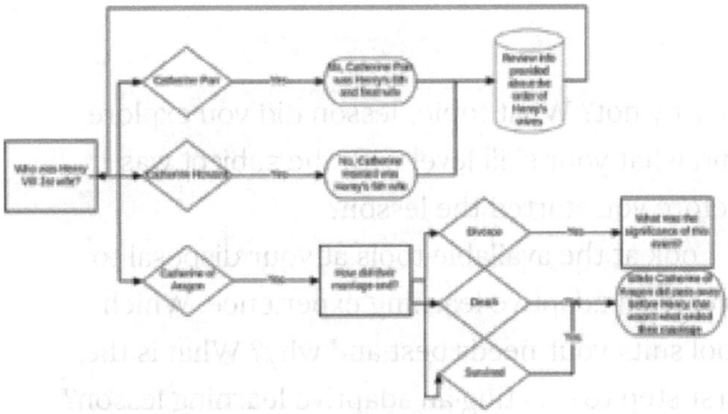

Figure 3: Henry VIII branching logic example for an adaptive learning strategy.

Questions for Discussion

1. What does Adaptive Learning mean to you? How would Adaptive Learning fit into your organization's teaching and learning framework?
2. Identify a tool that you could use to create an adaptive learning experience. Why did you pick this tool? Is it free? Is it easy to use? Is it already available at work? What makes this tool adaptive? What kind of learning experiences can you build with it?
3. Choose a topic at the Khan Academy website (https://www.khanacademy.org/) or explore a site like Duolingo (https://www.duolingo.com/). Take about 20 minutes to complete a lesson or two of your choice. What was the adaptive experience like? Could you tell that the system was adapting to your learning needs? As a student do you feel that this helped you learn more? Why

or why not? What topic/lesson did you explore and what your skill level with the subject was before you started the lesson?

4. Look at the available tools at your disposal to create an adaptive learning experience. Which tool suits your needs best and why? What is the first step to creating an adaptive learning lesson?
5. Reflection: Evaluate the game or simulation you have chosen to play. What are the pros and cons of this game or simulation? Would you recommend it to a friend? Why or why not? Does it satisfy your needs as a game player, based on your Bartle's Test results?

Recommended Supplementary Material

- Kerr, P. (2016). Adaptive learning. *ELT Journal*, 70(1), 88-93. https://doi.org/10.1093/elt/ccv055
- Essa, A. (2016). A possible future for next generation adaptive learning systems. *Smart Learning Environments*, 3(1), 1-24. https://doi.org/10.1186/s40561-016-0038-y
- Shedding Light on the Adaptive Black Box: Adaptive Learning Close Up

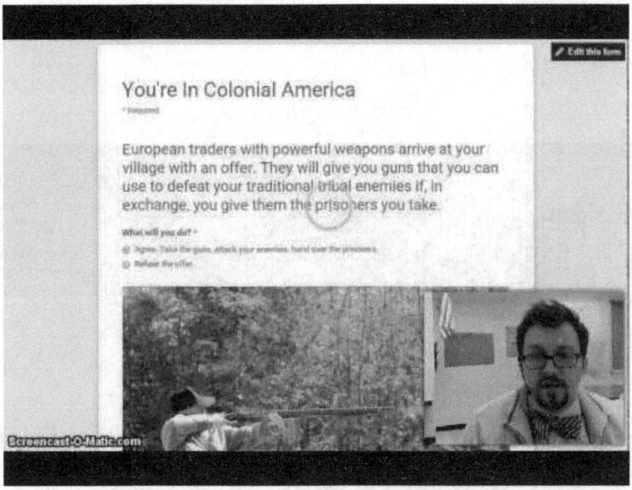

- *A YouTube element has been excluded from this version of the text. You can view it online here: https://mlpp.pressbooks.pub/gamebasedlearning/?p=30*

You Are Not So Smart Podcast, Episode 053 – Adaptive Learning – Ulrik Christensen

5. Differentiated Instruction

Learning Objectives

- Explain Adaptive Learning
- Recommend Adaptive Learning Solutions for your own organizational context
- Identify tools for use to create adaptive learning experiences
- Create a -Mini Adaptive Learning Experience
- Plan multiple methods of creating adaptive learning experiences

Differentiated instruction is a method that allows instructors to create avenues to learning content and assessment that speak to individual differences between students. In order to differentiate instruction and assessment, instructors or trainers must fully understand each student and their learning preferences. The idea behind differentiation goes back to the notion of personalized pathways to learning. Differentiation, unlike Adaptive Learning, doesn't necessarily require the use of technology to be implemented. Yet, like adaptive learning, differentiation is about information input and providing multiple approaches to exploring content.

By using Bloom's taxonomy to help design content exploration activities and assessments, instructional designers can offer learning experiences at multiple cognitive domains. For example, going back to our Henry VIII example, some differentiated activities for exploring the content might include:

- Ordering a list of Henry VIII's wives from first to last
- Reading a text or watching a video about Henry's wives and responding to questions
- Creating a Tudor family tree
- Presenting a summary of each wife and the political implications of each marriage to the monarchy

Differentiation also focuses on providing multiple avenues of information input. Giving students the opportunity to learn according to their learning *preference* can increase their motivation and engagement with the content. Providing the same or similar information via text, video, lecture, and/or interactive elearning module creates options for learners to satisfy and perhaps strengthen their multiple intelligences (Gardner, 2008).

When it comes to assessment, differentiation means offering learners multiple methods of expressing what they know. Aligning the assessments to the learning objectives is vital, but the format of the artifact a student produces can take many forms. Moving beyond essays and presentations both encourages student creativity and provides the learner with a more definitive demonstration of their skill or knowledge.

Differentiated Instruction is at the heart of adaptive learning, which is in turn, often an integral part of Game-Based Learning. At the core of each is the concept of personalizing and individualizing instruction in order to give the learner the best learning experience. The relationship between Differentiation, Adaptive Learning, and Game-Based Learning is illustrated in Figure 4 below.

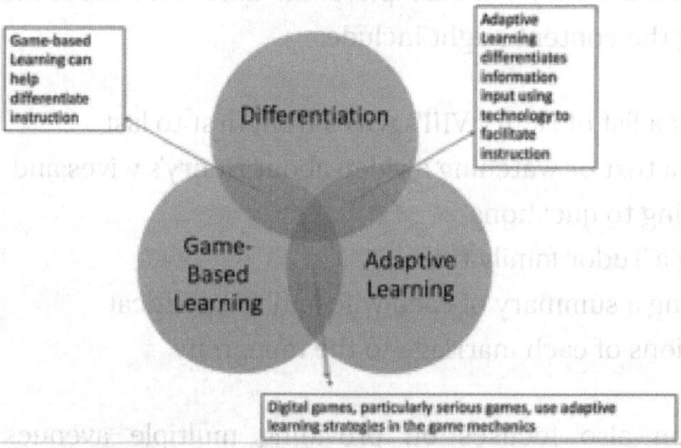

Figure 4: Venn Diagram of the overlap and differences of differentiation, adaptive learning, and game-based learning.

References

Gardner, H. E. (2008). *Multiple intelligences: New horizons in theory and practice*. Basic books.

Recommended Supplementary Material

- Taylor, B. K. (2015). Content, process, and product: Modeling differentiated instruction. *Kappa Delta Pi Record*, 51(1), 13-17. https://doi.org/10.1080/00228958.2015.988559
- Jennifer Gonzalez and Tracy Enos: Using Playlists to Differentiate Instruction

6. Personalized Learning

Learning Objectives

- Explain Adaptive Learning
- Recommend Adaptive Learning Solutions for your own organizational context
- Identify tools for use to create adaptive learning experiences
- Create a -Mini Adaptive Learning Experience
- Plan multiple methods of creating adaptive learning experiences

Personalized learning is a methodology which factors the learner's strengths, needs, personal interests, and learning goals, into one learning environment. The term is often used synonymously with differentiation but there is a key difference between the two. Personalized learning gives learners agency over their own learning experience because personalized learning takes their needs and their own learning goals into account.

An operational definition of personalized learning was proposed by a group of organizations that have interests and or investments in education, such as the Bill & Melinda Gates Foundation. This definition included elements such as a learner profile, a personal learning path, a competency-based curriculum, and a flexible learning environment (Cavanagh, 2014).

This approach, as with all student-centered approaches, requires the instructor to be a facilitator or guide rather than information giver. Methods, such as project-based learning, problem-based learning, or case-based learning are often used as content exploration methods under a personalized learning system.

In a personalized learning system, it is vital to understand learners' prior knowledge as well as their strengths and academic weaknesses. As instructional designers, building in both self-assessments and opportunities for students and instructors to define the learners' prior knowledge is vital to developing both the learner profile and the learning pathway.

The main component of personalized learning is the idea that the learners should have a sense of control over their own learning experience. Learner agency is created by the collaborative efforts of learner and instructor in defining learning goals and a path to those goals. Giving learners a voice in how they reach those goals empowers them and involves them in their own learning process. Combined with a flexible learning environment that gives them options in demonstrating competence or mastery over the learning goals is essential to this method.

Differentiation and performance assessment are both key components in creating these flexible learning environments. Technology is also making personalized learning more feasible for both instructors and students in all types of learning environments.

References

Cavanagh, S. (2014). What is "personalized learning"? Educators seek clarity. *Education Week*, 34(9), S2-S4.

Recommended Supplementary Material

- Feldstein, M., & Hill, P. (2016). Personalized

learning: What it really IS and why it really matters. EDUCAUSE *Review*, 51(2), 24. http://er.educause.edu/articles/2016/3/personalized-learning-what-it-really-is-and-why-it-really-matters

- *A TED element has been excluded from this version of the text. You can view it online here: https://mlpp.pressbooks.pub/gamebasedlearning/?p=34*

- *Warning – Contains Simulated Video Game Violence*

- *A YouTube element has been excluded from this version of the text. You can view it online here: https://mlpp.pressbooks.pub/gamebasedlearning/?p=34*

PART II

CHAPTER 2 - GAMES IN EDUCATION

7. Digital Games

Learning Objectives

- Summarize the current availability of serious games and digital games for educational purposes
- Select 2-3 digital games for potential use in your own organizational context

Learning engagement, motivation, problem-solving, logic practice, and risk-free exploration of the content are all benefits of using games in learning (Gee, 2010; Hainey et al., 2013; Lewis et al., 2013).

Digital games are games played on a computer, game system, television, or mobile device. They can be made specifically for educational purposes, in which case they are often referred to as "Serious Games," or they can be commercial games such as *Halo*, *Call of Duty*, or *Hearthstone*.

Digital games can be designed for single-player, online, co-op, or collaborative play. Some digital games, such as *Final Fantasy* XI or *EverQuest*, fall into the Massive Multiplayer Online (MMO) category, meaning that players worldwide log in to a virtual world to play the game.

Digital games fall into many categories. Role-playing games (RPGs), first-person shooters (FPS), social games, sports games, casual games, racing games, music games, and combat games are types of digital games that have very different game mechanics, goals, and gameplay.

Gaming Software in education is a growing platform that allows students to acquire knowledge in various subjects through reaching specific game objectives on their electronic devices. Here are a few platforms that would allow you to create your own games or simulations:

GameSalad – GameSalad is a platform that allows users to create 2D games with no programming.

Twine – Twine is a free, text-based game creator geared for those who would like to create Interactive Fiction

Gamestar Mechanic – Gamestar Mechanic uses fun, game-based quests and courses to help you learn game design and make your own video games!

Unity – A real-time game development platform that allows you to create 3D, 2D, VR & AR experiences.

Digital Game Sources

iCivics

iCivics is non-profit organization driven by Justice Sandra Day O'Connor's passion for increasing civics knowledge in K-12 students. iCivics and Filament Games have developed a suite of games and lesson plans based on various civics and governmental topics.

Filament Games

Filament Games produces games exclusively for learning, relying on their staff of instructional designers and game developers to create games that are based on learning theory.

Center for Games and Impact

The Center for Games and Impact at Arizona State University is the brainchild of Dr. James Gee, one of the top names in educational gaming. The Center's mission is to evaluate the impact of games on learning and evaluate the sustainability of gaming models in education.

OpenSimulator

OpenSimulator is an open platform sim creator that can be used to create a virtual environment.

Making History

The Making History games series provides players an opportunity to work through alternate history events using logic and strategy to determine the course of events for their chosen country.

Getbadnews.com

Get as many followers as you can by creating fake news.

Fake it to make it

A social impact game about fake news.

This War of Mine

Try to survive in a city under siege

References

Gee, J. P. (2010). Video games: What they can teach us about audience engagement. *Nieman Reports*, 64(2), 52.

Hainey, T., Westera, W., Connolly, T. M., Boyle, L., Baxter, G., Beeby, R. B., & Soflano, M. (2013). Students' attitudes toward playing games and using games in education: Comparing Scotland and the Netherlands. *Computers & Education*, 69, 474.

Lewis, C., Lancaster, J., Savenye, W., & Haas, N. (2013). A formative evaluation of the balance of power game and curriculum. *Journal of Applied Instructional Design*, 3(3), 5-16. https://docs.wixstatic.com/ugd/c9b0ce_3456d4cf26e94d7c9c39ae1012d62907.pdf

Recommended Supplementary Material

- Ariffin, M. M., Oxley, A., & Sulaiman, S. (2014). Evaluating game-based learning effectiveness in higher education. Procedia – Social and Behavioral Sciences, 123, 20-27. https://doi.org/10.1016/

j.sbspro.2014.01.1393

- Gee, J. P. (2013). Games for learning. *Educational Horizons*, 91(4), 16-20. http://journals.sagepub.com/doi/full/10.1177/0013175X1309100406

- *A TED element has been excluded from this version of the text. You can view it online here: https://mlpp.pressbooks.pub/gamebasedlearning/?p=36*

- https://www.legendsoflearning.com/

8. Serious Games

Learning Objectives

- Summarize the current availability of serious games and digital games for educational purposes
- Select 2-3 digital games for potential use in your own organizational context

Serious games are digital games designed specifically for learning or for another purpose than entertainment. These games can be used for education and learning purposes or for on-the-job training. Companies such as Little Bird Games, Filament Games, and Designing Digitally have a portfolio of games created for just those reasons.

Serious games employ game mechanics (stories, interactivity, rules, challenges, competition, risks) to topics with "serious" agendas. One example is the game *Cashier Trainer*, designed to give new hires training on job duties and register functions before going out into the workplace. Results of a study comparing the game to conventional on-the-job training showed that new hires in the *Cashier Trainer* game group performed as high or higher on a final skills test (Oprins & Korteling, 2014).

As a part of the serious game movement, Augmented Reality (AR) and Virtual Reality (VR) have become a part of the digital educational experience. Augmented Reality harnesses the power of tools we have at our fingertips, such as Smartphones and Tablets, and uses programming to superimpose computer-generated images over images of the real world. Examples of AR include the apps Curiscope and Star Walk, both of which allow users to explore 3D images and interact with the content. Virtual Reality (VR) uses special technology tools, such as Oculus Rift glasses, to immerse the user in a computer-generated world. Often, VR headsets will be paired with gloves or full helmets that include sensors to give the user a fully tactile experience. zSpace, Alchemy Immersive, and Google Expeditions are all sites dedicated to the use of VR in education.

Serious games are often built using programs such as Unity 3D. Most game design platforms require a basic knowledge of programming languages, but some such as Twine or GameStar Mechanic are better for users who do not want to code.

Questions for Discussion

1. Choose either the pro or con for the use of digital and serious games in learning. Explain your stance in the discussion while considering the following questions: Is this trend a positive or negative for learners? What evidence can we find in academic studies to support your argument? What is the current state of serious and digital games for educational purposes? How does that fit in with your thesis?
2. Using the impact guides at the Center for Games and Impact (https://gamesandimpact.org/impact-guides/), select 2-3 digital or serious games that could be used in an educational

context that you are familiar with. Explain why you chose those games and how they fit into teaching and learning in your organization.

References

Oprins, E. B. E., & Korteling, J. H. (2014). Transfer of training of an educational serious game: The effectiveness of the CASHIER TRAINER. In *Simulations, Serious Games and Their Applications* (pp. 227-253). Springer: Singapore.

Recommended Supplementary Material

- De Lope, R. P., & Medina Medina, N. (2016). A comprehensive taxonomy for serious games. *Journal of Educational Computing Research.* https://doi.org/10.1177/0735633116681301
- Game and Learn Podcast by Dr. Ruben Puentedura (episode 13: Serious Games https://itunes.apple.com/us/podcast/serious-games/id429426265?i=1000092588134&mt=2)

9. Non-Digital Games

Learning Objectives

- Describe the use of non-digital games in educational or training contexts
- Create a non-digital game solution to an educational or training problem

Non-digital games, also known as analog games, are any type of game that is not played on a digital device (computer, game console, phone, or tablet). Board games, card games, and sports games are examples of non-digital games.

Implementing non-digital games into a learning experience can be much cheaper and faster than attempting a serious or other digital game. Some non-digital games require nothing more than a piece of paper and a pencil, such as BINGO. Commercial board games can be adapted to suit the content or can be recreated using the same game mechanics and appearance of a game. Card games make great review strategies and there are currently many commercial card games available that can serve that purpose, such as Miles Bornes or Memory.

Non-digital games can be exciting and creative ways for your students to express their understanding of the content. Game creation as an assessment option offers learners opportunities to reach higher cognitive domain levels on Bloom's Taxonomy while demonstrating what they have learned. In addition, encouraging students to play one another's games is a great way to build communities of learning.

Empirical studies around the use of non-digital games, such as board games, in learning environments, show that students achieve higher learning gains and have a higher rate of satisfaction with the learning experience (Anyanwu, 2014; Lee et al., 2015).

Possibly the greatest benefit to non-digital games is that they can be played anywhere. Whether your organization has a budget or not, whether your learners have access to technology or not, non-digital games are a way to implement Game-Based Learning without money or technology concerns. Learners can take the games with them for on-the-go revision or they can play the game outside of training or classroom time with their co-workers or classmates.

A quick Google search will turn up a host of blank board game templates that you can use to create your own game. You can also turn your training or classroom into a game using paper and everyday items as in the Candyland library room pictured in Figure 5.

Figure 5. Manchester City Library. "Life-Sized Candyland". 15 March, 2010. Online image. Flikr. https://flic.kr/p/7L1hLw. (CC BY-SA 2.0)

Questions for Discussion

1. Make a case for the use of non-digital games as learning tools within your organization. As an instructional designer, how can you advocate for the use of non-digital games? Is there a particular learning context in which non-digital games would fit? What evidence can you provide (or cite) that will help convince others in your organization to use non-digital games?
2. Reflection: What is your favorite non-digital game? How often do you play? With whom do you play? Is this different from your routine digital gameplay? Why or why not?

References

Anyanwu, E. G. (2014). Anatomy adventure: A board game for enhancing understanding of anatomy. *Anatomical Sciences Education*, 7(2), 153-160.

Lee, E., Moreau, K., & Lochnan, H. (2015). A customised board game enhances learning about obesity. *Medical education*, 49(11), 1149-1150.

Recommended Supplementary Material

- Khan, A., & Pearce, G. (2015). A study into the effects of a board game on flow in undergraduate business students. *The International Journal of Management Education*, 13(3), 193-201. https://doi.org/10.1016/j.ijme.2015.05.002

- *A TED element has been excluded from this version of the text. You can view it online here: https://mlpp.pressbooks.pub/gamebasedlearning/?p=60*

- *Warning – Contains Simulated Video Game Violence*

- *A YouTube element has been excluded from this version of the text. You can view it online here: https://mlpp.pressbooks.pub/gamebasedlearning/?p=60*

10. Play Theory

> *"We don't stop playing because we grow old; we grow old because we stop playing." ~George Bernard Shaw*

Play theory generally refers to cognitive development in younger children. Building off of Vygotsky's theory of cognition, Play Theory hypothesizes that play is an important component of both language development and understanding the external world as children play, and role play, situations to find solutions. The social interaction of children's play increases their learning as they experiment, fail, receive feedback, revise their strategies, and reattempt play. Problem-solving, therefore, is an essential part of play that allows the child to hone their performance during play. Imaginative play is also important to cognitive development because it allows children to enhance their language and problem-solving skills.

If we look at game mechanics and the elements that are present in most games, we will see an overlap with play theory. Experiment, failing, receiving feedback, revising strategies, and reattempting play are all components of games.

What differences do you see between play and games?

Although Play Theory is generally used in reference to Early Childhood Education, clear parallels exist between Play Theory and Game-Based Learning. Play, whether it is gameplay or other forms of play, creates an environment of low-pressure learning, allowing for failure to become a learning opportunity. Play creates trust and relationships, increasing cooperation and collaboration. Play also enhances creativity and innovative thinking through problem-solving and the use of imaginative strategies. In adult learning experiences, play can create an environment of "fun, spontaneity, relationship and connection, silliness or goofiness, creativity, and imagination. Furthermore, play and playfulness were most frequently manifested in the classroom through risk-taking, storytelling, and physical activities" (Tanis, 2012, p. iii).

References

Tanis, D. J. (2012). Exploring play/playfulness and learning in the adult and higher education classroom.

Recommended Supplementary Material

- Mercer, T. G., Kythreotis, A. P., Stolte, T., Robinson, Z. P., George, S. M., & Haywood, S. K. (2017). The Use of Educational Game Design and Play in Higher Education to Influence Sustainable Behaviour. *International Journal of Sustainability in Higher Education*, 18(3).

- *A TED element has been excluded from this*

version of the text. You can view it online here: https://mlpp.pressbooks.pub/gamebasedlearning/?p=62

11. Commercial Games

Learning Objectives

- Debate the impact of commercial games for education and training
- Evaluate commercially available games for use in educational contexts

From *Where in the World is Carmen Sandiego?* to *Minecraft*, commercial games have long been used in educational settings. As commercial video games and video game platforms advance at a rapid pace, can we still make the argument that games such as *Call of Duty*, *Elven Scrolls*, or *Clash of Clans* are useful in educational settings? GBL experts, like Jim Gee and Elisabeth Hayes, would argue that indeed we can! Gee and Hayes (2010) make the argument that commercial video games develop academic literacy in players – meaning they teach people how to learn. In studies, Gee and Hayes (2010) have shown that commercial video games can also help players, and female players, in particular, develop a socioemotional intelligence through collaboration, creative problem solving, and artistic creation.

If we think about any video games you may have played, or the game you are playing now, reflect on how you learned the ins and outs of gameplay. Was there a tutorial? Were there instructions? Gone are the days of a game disc jacket with game instructions. Commercial video games now offer learning levels and in-game learning opportunities. How do you know how to upgrade your character's strengths? How do you determine what tasks to undertake first? The "unlearned" lessons in gameplay are instilling academic literacy – they are teaching you how to learn within the context of the game by encouraging exploration and experimentation.

By using commercial video games in educational settings, we can create an environment where conversations about metacognition, a critical awareness of how we as individuals think and learn, are natural extensions of the course activities. There is much evidence to suggest the efficacy of using commercial games in K-12 education but there is much less information about the use of commercial games in higher education or in training outside of military training or medical training. There is research evidence to support the use of commercial video games as pre-operative warm-ups for surgeons (Jalink et al., 2015).

But what else can commercial games teach our students? Commercial games by definition include digital and board games. What makes a game worth the purchase price? Here are some of the skills that commercial games, both digital and board, can encourage in your learners:

- Literacy
- Communication
- Team-work
- Problem-solving
- Forecasting
- Strategic thinking

In addition to the skills listed above, there can be some value in correcting content mistakes. History students playing *Assassin's Creed* may be able to spot historical inaccuracies in the storyline. Literature students can compare the *Lord of the Rings* video games to the books and evaluate how a change in a character's actions changes the storyline. Video games with strong female characters, like *Tomb Raider* or *Resident Evil*, can be a launch point for discussions on feminism, gender equality, and body image.

Questions for Discussion

1. Revisit the available Impact Guides from Arizona State's Center for Games and Impact (https://gamesandimpact.org/impact-guides/). Choose at least two games and review any and all impact guides for each one. What, if anything, is missing from the guides? What benefit do these guides provide to users? Can you see yourself using the existing guides or designing your own if you choose to implement commercial games into learning? Did these guides sway your views on the value of commercial games in education? Why or why not?
2. Based on the readings, how do you feel about commercial games in educational contexts? Is there evidence to challenge the use of commercial video games in learning?

References

Gee, J., & Hayes, E. R. (2010). *Women and gaming: The Sims and 21st-century learning*. Springer.

Jalink, M. B., Heineman, E., Pierie, J. P. E. N., & ten Cate Hoedemaker, H. O. (2015). The effect of a preoperative warm-up with a custom-made Nintendo video game on the performance of laparoscopic surgeons. *Surgical Endoscopy*, 29(8), 2284-2290.

Recommended Supplementary Material

- Kühn, S., Gleich, T., Lorenz, R. C., Lindenberger, U., & Gallinat, J. (2014). Playing super mario induces structural brain plasticity: Gray matter changes resulting from training with a commercial video game. *Molecular Psychiatry*, 19(2), 265-71. http://dx.doi.org/10.1038/mp.2013.120
- Ramsay, D. (2015). Brutal games: Call of duty and the cultural narrative of world war II. *Cinema Journal*, 54(2), 94-113. Retrieved from http://ezproxy.mnsu.edu/login?url=http://search.proquest.com/docview/1760208166?accountid=12259
- Copp, S. E., Fischer, R. L., Luo, T., Moore, D. R., & Dikkers, S. (2014). Analyzing Commercial Video Game Instruction through the Lens of Instructional Design. *Journal of Applied Instructional Design*, 4(1), 79-90.
- Ed Got Game Podcast #19 The Good, Bad and the Ugly of Using Commercial Games in the Classroom

- *A YouTube element has been excluded from this version of the text. You can view it online here: https://mlpp.pressbooks.pub/gamebasedlearning/?p=64*

PART III

CHAPTER 3 - SIMULATIONS

12. High-Fidelity Simulations

Learning Objectives

- Distinguish between high-fidelity and digital simulations
- Describe opportunities to integrate simulations into educational contexts

Simulations are created situations that mimic real-life situations that learners are likely to encounter in the content area. Simulations are highly used in medical education, military training, and machinery training. Simulations can vary in their fidelity level or their similarity to real-life situations.

High-fidelity simulations are the most realistic and are used heavily to train nurses and doctors. They are also being used to train law enforcement officers. High-fidelity simulations, as shown in Figures 6-7, often require the use of actors or hidden participants that act as voices or controllers of mannequins.

Figure 6: High-fidelity law enforcement simulation with three officer trainees and an instructor "acting" as a disruptive bar patron.

High-fidelity simulations often require investments in equipment, technology, and personnel due to the realistic nature of the scenarios. The benefits to the investment in labs or simulation rooms include the increase in skill transfer to real-life scenarios and the opportunity for review and reflection as a post-action report. Often, simulations are recorded and participants have the opportunity to review their performance with their instructors to receive feedback and clarification.

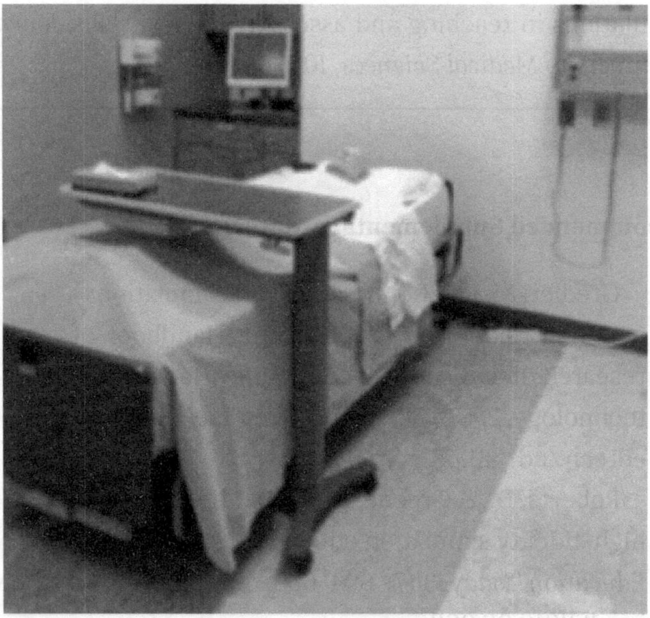

Figure 7: High-fidelity nursing simulation with an electronic mannequin. The mannequin includes a speaker that can be voiced by an instructor or actor from a control booth.

Studies have shown mixed results on the efficacy of high-fidelity versus low-fidelity simulations (Munshi et al., 2015). However, evidence points to the efficiency of simulations in general for increasing learning gains. The essential elements in any simulation include opportunities for feedback, repetition of skills, and relevance to the curriculum. Researchers in the area of high-fidelity simulations suggest that the largest benefit to the use of high-fidelity simulations is in increasing learner self-efficacy and allowing them to demonstrate to themselves that they can perform the skills they are learning (Dunn et al., 2014).

References

Dunn, K. E., Osborne, C., & Link, H. J. (2014). Research briefs high-fidelity simulation and nursing student self-efficacy: Does training help the little engines know they can? *Nursing Education Perspectives*, 35(6), 403-404.

Munshi, F., Lababidi, H., & Alyousef, S. (2015). Low-versus high-fidelity simulations in teaching and assessing clinical skills. *Journal of Taibah University Medical Sciences*, 10(1), 12-15.

Recommended Supplementary Material

- Gredler, M. E. (2004). Games and simulations and their relationships to learning. Handbook of research on educational communications and technology, 2, 571-581. http://www.aect.org/edtech/ed1/21.pdf
- Roberts, D., & Greene, L. (2011). The theatre of high-fidelity simulation education. *Nurse Education Today*, 31(7), 694-698. doi:10.1016/j.nedt.2010.06.003

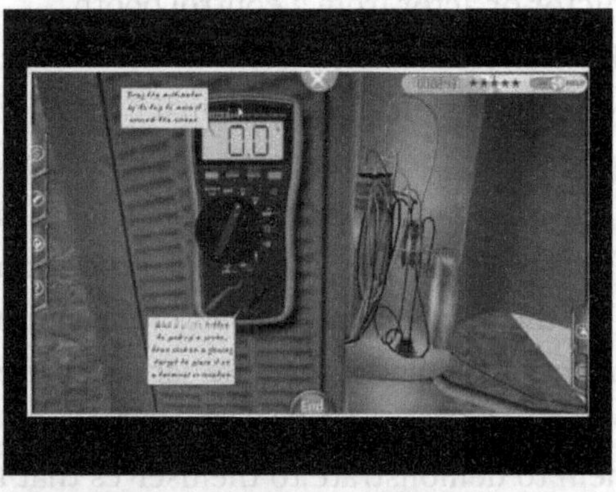

- *A YouTube element has been excluded from this version of the text. You can view it online here: https://mlpp.pressbooks.pub/gamebasedlearning/?p=68*

13. Digital Simulations

Learning Objectives

- Distinguish between high-fidelity and digital simulations
- Describe opportunities to integrate simulations into educational contexts

Digital simulations are computer-based versions of high-fidelity simulations. Rather than going into a lab and role-playing skills, learners interact in a virtual environment to practice those same skills. Digital simulations are often used as precursors to high-fidelity simulations, scaffolding the learning environment from relatively low interactivity to higher interactivity. Digital simulations are often used to train operators of heavy machinery or vehicles, such as tanks, front loaders, and other construction equipment. Digital simulations are also used to prepare learners in trade programs for using welding and HVAC equipment. Some digital simulations are used to introduce learners to new software or technology tools in the workplace.

Like high-fidelity simulations, digital simulations promote skill transfer and learner self-efficacy. In a detailed review of the literature, Gegenfurtner, Quesada-Pallarès, and Knogler (2014) found that when developing digital simulations, instructional designers should focus on the user control aspect of the simulation over elements such as social, narrative, or multimedia. In other words, unlike a video game, a simulation doesn't necessarily need a good story, fancy multimedia interactions, or collaboration opportunities with other users. Additionally, these authors found that assessment after training was a vital piece of the success of using digital simulations effectively for learning and increasing the likelihood of skill transfer.

Nestled into a small aspect of digital simulations is education within virtual worlds, such as Second Life. While Second Life (SL) is not designed specifically for education, some institutions have chosen to purchase "islands" in SL and host online classes within the virtual world. Some teachers and institutions have created virtual learning environments around their content such as a complete replica of a Mexican village or Macbeth's castle. The benefit of learning in the real world, particularly for language instruction, is the authentic interaction that learners can have with the "residents" of SL, who are logged on from all over the globe. Spanish students can log in to SL and listen to a live flamenco concert or converse with native Spanish speakers.

The popularity of Second Life for educational purposes has waned over the last few years. The expense of maintaining an island or space in SL is large and concerns about learners' digital safety were sufficient enough to discourage most educators from continuing the explorations of SL as a learning tool. However, there is still some educational presence from larger universities. We will learn more about SL and other virtual worlds in Week 10.

Digital simulations can be useful in helping students understand abstract concepts. For physics students, a simulation like *Supercharged!* helps learners visualize ion and particle charges and how they work together. Simulations like *Volcano Island* allow students to manipulate a geologic environment to determine what forces cause volcanic eruptions.

Questions for Discussion

1. What type of simulation might be the best choice for your particular organization? Why? What would this simulation be used for?
2. Reflection: Based on what you've learned so far, in your opinion, what is the value of games and simulations in education? How can they be used effectively, if at all?

References

Gegenfurtner, A., Quesada-Pallarès, C., & Knogler, M. (2014). Digital simulation-based training: A meta-analysis. *British Journal of Educational Technology*, 45(6), 1097-1114.

Recommended Supplementary Material

- Balasubramanian, N., & Wilson, B. G. (2005). Games and simulations. ForeSITE, 1. http://www.coulthard.com/library/Files/balasubramanianwilson_2005-gamesandsimulations.pdf

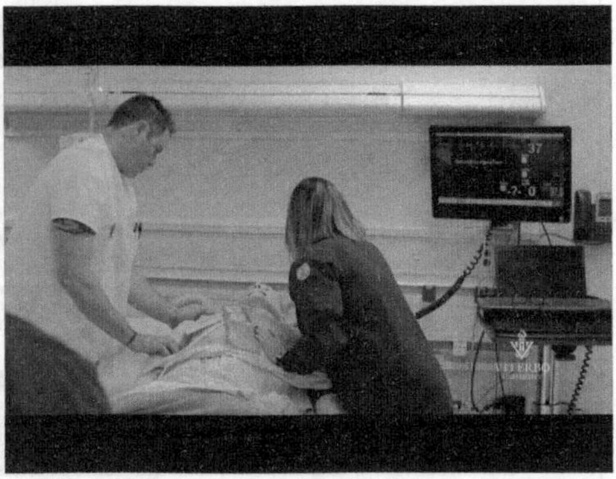

- *A YouTube element has been excluded from this version of the text. You can view it online here: https://mlpp.pressbooks.pub/gamebasedlearning/?p=70*

- *Warning – Contains Simulated Video Game Violence*

- *A YouTube element has been excluded from this version of the text. You can view it online here: https://mlpp.pressbooks.pub/gamebasedlearning/?p=70*

PART IV

CHAPTER 4 - GAMIFICATION

14. Gamification

15. Steps for Gamifying a Learning Experience

1. **Change the Vocabulary**

The first step to gamifying a learning experience is to create the environment of a game. Changing the vocabulary of a learning experience to that of a game will help set the stage and assist in learner buy-in. Some examples of vocabulary changes are:

- Modules / weeks / units -> Levels / quests / rooms / maps
- Grades / Grade points -> XP ("experience points") / gold bars/ achievements
- Groups -> Guilds / Clans / Tribes
- Assignments -> Quests / Journeys

2. **Create the Context**

Good games have great storylines that give players a context for why they are completing difficult quests and arduous journeys. Create the same feeling in your learning experience by developing a storyline for the content. Are the learners completing a mission to Mars? A wagon train out west? Are they on a wilderness expedition or part of a multi-national conglomerate? Maybe they are superheroes or simply fantasy characters (wizards, mages, Vikings, hunters, etc.).

Whatever the story is, create the context and carry it through all aspects of the learning experience including the syllabus and the assignment descriptions. For example, if the learners will be going on a Mission to Mars, the instructor should be the Mission

Commander or the Base Commander. Assignments can be Cadet Missions. Grades can be miles completed towards the Mars landing.

3. **Create a Ranking Structure**

Once you have the story, create a ranking structure based on likely characters in your scenario. Using the Mission to Mars example, incoming learners to the learning experience might be Cadets. As they earn "miles" towards the goal, they can progress in rank:

- Cadet
- Flight Engineer
- Mission Specialist
- Pilot
- Commander

Not only will these rankings help in Leaderboard creation, but you can give them meaning if the instructor assigns students to group work or discussions, assigning students of different "ranks" various roles.

4. **Use the tools at hand**

Most learning management systems include many tools that can add gamification elements to a learning experience. While each LMS is different, exploring the features and tools of your specific learning management system may turn up some useful items to use in gamifying a learning experience. Here are some ideas to look for:

- **Automated emails** – send "bonus" or achievement notifications to students who complete designated tasks
- **Checklists** – allows students to see the tasks they need to complete in order to "level up"
- **Release conditions or branching logic** – allows content to be released based on "gameplay" and achievements
- **Groups tool** – allows students to function within a community

in their different roles. Rename the individual groups as students choose names for their "guild" or "clan."

- **Discussion Board tools** – Up-voting features allow students to choose group names or vote on discussions. Individual discussion forums could be created as "base camps" for one-on-one student interaction.
- **Widgets** – add leaderboards to your course homepage or include relevant game elements like a "help menu" can further your game feel
- **Embeddable videos** in discussions, content, and news items – allows you to add context and story elements to the course
- **Grades** – create hidden bonus items that unlock based on release conditions
- **Modules** – create "easter egg" items such as study guides or helpful resources that unlock based on release conditions
- **Badges and Awards** – tie a badge or certificate to an individual assignment or task

5. **Include Personalization**

Allowing learners to choose avatars will help anonymize the leaderboard, but you can take it one step further. Allow groups to choose group names and use those names to title group discussions or assignments. Let learners decide what type of character they will be in the game – wizard, mage, guardian, warrior – and let that drive their assignment submissions. You can use tools like the *Bartle Test of Gamer Psychology* to build groups or help students decide what type of gamer they are.

6. **Encourage instructors to stay up to date**

One of the fundamental aspects of gaming is the sense of community, competition, and accomplishment. Keeping grades, and therefore leaderboards, as up-to-date as possible is important for maintaining learner motivation.

7. **Create a support structure from the beginning**

At the beginning of the course, let learners know how the course will be structured and provide them with an overview of the gameplay. Add in some gamification resources and prepare the instructor for questions, perhaps by creating an FAQ document. It is very common for learners to struggle with the change in vocabulary and environment that gamification brings. Let them know it is ok not to like games, but that it is important to keep an open mind. Allow learners to opt out of things like the leaderboard or even gameplay if possible.

8. **Differentiate assignments**

Part of the beauty of gameplay is that there are not always the same ways to achieve results. Offer your learners multiple paths to the same end goal – if you usually create a paper writing assignment, give them the option to create a multimedia presentation, blog, podcast, or video.

9. **Issue Challenges**

If you choose to gamify an entire learning experience, rather than just a lesson, don't let the gameplay become boring or routine once you hit the mid-point of the learning experience. Hide challenges, the possibility for bonus points, or additional easter eggs to keep the game momentum moving.

10. **Designate a "Winner"**

Create a structure so that the instructor can use the leaderboard and the final grades to let the winner(s) of the "game" know that they won. The instructor can assign bonus points, a badge, a certificate, or just send them a message with a "You Won!" notification. Using automated emails is a great tool for this game element.

16. Badging

Learning Objectives

- Summarize the benefits and challenges of implementing a badging system
- Identify badging platforms
- Create 3-4 badges for a learning experience that the learners are familiar with

A badge is a symbol or indicator of an accomplishment of skills, qualities, or interests, and they are a digital way to acknowledge student work or their accomplishments. For example, students might receive a badge if they achieve certain levels of success on assignments or if they do extra work, such as learning a new grammatical concept or editing another student's work. Learners in the class can see other students' badges so that they will be encouraged to compete and be aware of the different badges that can be earned. For teachers, badges make classroom goals more visible to students. Badges can have a significant impact on motivating learners to participate and collaborate, and can also be used as an assessment tool. Figure 8 shows examples of badges that were created and awarded to students in a game-based learning in education course.

Figure 8. Example badges students were awarded in a GBL in Education course.

Badging is not a new concept to motivation and achievement. Scouting badges have been issued for over a century and many organizations issue physical badges to reward exceptional employee performance (Figures 9-10).

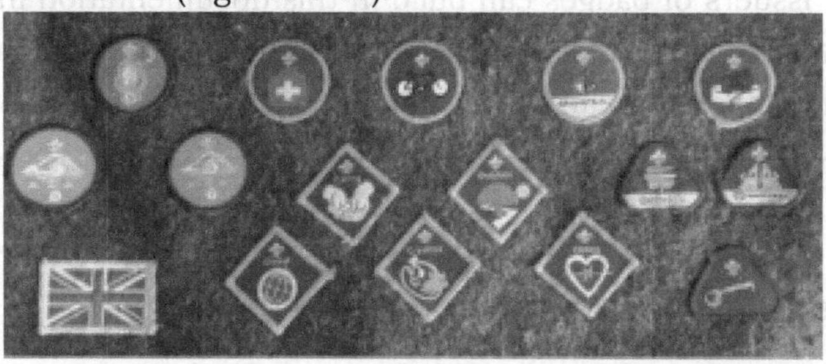

Figure 9. Scouting badges. From "Cubs badge selection" by Rafmarham, 2020, https://commons.wikimedia.org/wiki/File:Cubs_badge_selection.jpg#file. CC-BY-SA-4.0

Figure 10. Merit badges issued by the Home Depot to employees.

Digital badges are electronic symbols used as credentialing tools that serve as a visual representation of knowledge or skills that have been obtained or completed. Often called "micro-credentials", badges are often awarded at the end of training modules, conferences, or other professional development offerings (Stefaniak & Carey, 2019). Badge design and process of implementation depend on the purpose of the badge. Badges are issued by individual organizations that set criteria for what constitutes earning a badge. They're most often issued through an online credential or badging platforms such as Badgr or Accredible. These platforms allow organizations to design, issue, and manage the various badges they want to award to individuals. Badges can also be created using design programs or using badging tools within certain learning management systems (e.g., Brightspace, Canvas, Moodle). Open badges are a subset of digital badges that contain built-in data that provides "proof" to the viewer that the badge holder has earned that credential. Issuers of badges can build in this documentation into the badging platform so that when a badge is clicked on, the digital evidence of competency can be viewed.

Question for Discussion

1. Think of a learning context with which you are familiar. Using one of the free badging platforms, create 2-3 badges. Post them in a discussion and describe to use how you would use them. What in the readings supports your intended use of these badges? What design decisions did you make in terms of color, appearance, name, and evidence needed?

References

Stefaniak, J., & Carey, K. (2019). Instilling purpose and value in the implementation of digital badges in higher education. *Int J Educ Technol High Educ*, 16(44). https://doi.org/10.1186/s41239-019-0175-9

Recommended Supplementary Material

- Gamrat, C., Zimmerman, H. T., Dudek, J., & Peck, K. (2014). Personalized workplace learning: An exploratory study on digital badging within a teacher professional development program. *British Journal of Educational Technology*, 45(6), 1136-1148. https://doi.org/10.1111/bjet.12200
- Ford, E., Izumi, B., Lottes, J., & Richardson, D. (2015). Badge it. *Reference Services Review*, 43(1), 31-44. https://doi.org/10.1108/RSR-07-2014-0026
- Ahn, J., Pellicone, A., & Butler, B. S. (2014). Open badges for education: What are the implications at the intersection of open systems and badging? *Research in Learning Technology*, 22(1), 23563-13. https://doi.org/10.3402/rlt.v22.23563
- All about Digital Badges podcast by Connie Malamed, The eLearning Coach podcast https://itunes.apple.com/us/podcast/elc-022-all-about-digital-badges/id592110281?i=1000335943845&mt=2

PART V

CHAPTER 5 - VIRTUAL WORLDS

17. Virtual Worlds

Learning Objectives

- Define the term virtual worlds
- Identify examples of virtual world platforms
- Assess the digital safety concerns of implementing learning environments in virtual worlds

The discussion of virtual worlds as a part of Game-Based Learning tends to blur the line between virtual reality and video games. For example, Minecraft and World of Warcraft are both games but can also fall into the category of virtual worlds.

> "A *virtual world is a computer-based online community environment that is designed and shared by individuals so that they can interact in a custom-built, simulated world. Users interact with each other in this simulated world using text-based, two-dimensional or three-dimensional graphical models called avatars. Avatars are graphically rendered using computer graphics imaging (CGI) or any other rendering technology. Individuals control their avatars using input devices like the keyboard, mouse and other specially designed command and simulation gadgets. Today's virtual worlds are purpose-built for entertainment, social, educational, training and various other purposes.*
>
> *All virtual worlds possess the qualities of persistence and*

interactivity. This enables the users to explore the inherent benefits of socialization and allows them to study human nature and users' abilities.

A *virtual world may also be called a digital world.*" ("Virtual Worlds," 2017, para. 1-3)

Virtual worlds are generally designed to closely simulate real-life as much as possible. Once again, we see this blurry overlap – are virtual worlds simulations? Or are they games? Or are they a separate category altogether? The answer is all three. It largely depends on how the software is being employed that places it into a category. *The Sims* can be played for entertainment which makes it a game that is also a virtual world. Using it as a learning tool to discuss social interactions or run family or social experiments may move it into the realm of simulation.

Essentially, virtual worlds are a technology tool that can be used as entertainment or education. When Virtual Worlds are used for education, the results tend to be favorable. In a study of chemistry students using either a virtual lab inside Second Life or students using an in-person lab, those using the Second Life lab performed as well as the students using the in-person lab. Students indicated that they felt less distracted doing the experiment in Second Life and that certain components of the experiments were easier to do inside the virtual world (Winkelmann et al., 2020).

Other studies have found that the anonymity of learning in a virtual world and the use of avatars, actually encourages some students to participate. Particularly in the area of English as a Second Language, Chen and Kent (2020) found that students who participated in a virtual course held in Second Life provided more opportunities for the students to communicate spontaneously while engaged in real-world speaking tasks.

Questions for Discussion

1. Explore some of the various virtual world platforms. Which one(s) are you most interested in exploring, if any? What might appeal to learners about virtual worlds?
2. What specific safety concerns must we consider when designing educational interactions in virtual worlds?

References

Chen, J. C., & Kent, S. (2020). Task engagement, learner motivation and avatar identities of struggling English language learners in the 3D virtual world. *System*, 88, 102168.

Techopedia (2017). Virtual World. Retrieved from: https://www.techopedia.com/definition/25604/virtual-world

Winkelmann, K., Keeney-Kennicutt, W., Fowler, D., Lazo Macik, M., Perez Guarda, P., & Joan Ahlborn, C. (2020). Learning gains and attitudes of students performing chemistry experiments in an immersive virtual world. *Interactive Learning Environments*, 28(5), 620-634.

Suggested additional resources

- Fowler, C. (2015). Virtual reality and learning: Where is the pedagogy?: Learning activities in 3-D virtual worlds. *British Journal of Educational Technology*, 46(2), 412-422. https://doi.org/10.1111/

bjet.12135

- Lackey, S. J., Salcedo, J. N., Szalma, J. L., & Hancock, P. A. (2016). The stress and workload of virtual reality training: The effects of presence, immersion and flow. *Ergonomics*, 59(8), 1060-1072. https://doi.org/10.1080/00140139.2015.1122234
- Nussli, N. C., & Oh, K. (2015). A systematic, inquiry-based 7-step virtual worlds teacher training. *E-Learning and Digital Media*, 12(5-6), 502-529. https://doi.org/10.1177/2042753016672900

- *A YouTube element has been excluded from this version of the text. You can view it online here: https://mlpp.pressbooks.pub/gamebasedlearning/?p=83*

- *A YouTube element has been excluded from this version of the text. You can view it online here: https://mlpp.pressbooks.pub/gamebasedlearning/?p=83*

18. Virtual Reality

Learning Objectives

- Define Virtual Reality
- Identify options for integrating VR into learning environments

Virtual reality (VR) is similar to virtual worlds in that a user enters an immersive environment similar to real-life through the use of technology. However, unlike virtual worlds, virtual reality environments require special equipment, such as the Oculus Rift Goggles, in order to tap into sensory input. Goggles, helmets, gloves, haptic chairs, or sensors are placed on a user's person in order to fully immerse them in the virtual environment as shown in Figure 11. In education, virtual reality has yet to become mainstream for a variety of reasons including the cost of equipment. Google has launched *Google Expeditions* in combination with Google Cardboard, a device that turns any Android phone into VR goggles. *Google Expeditions* allows users to go on virtual field trips and experience the world right from their classroom. Sadly, *Google Expeditions* will be discontinued as of July 2021, but the created Expeditions will be saved to the Google Arts and Culture site.

Figure 11: Archeology student wearing VR goggles. Wessex Archeology. (Photographer). (2020, February 5). *Archeology in Virtual Reality!* [digital image].

Virtual reality has been used to train medical students on specific medical procedures (Labovitz, & Hubbard, 2020; Sattar et al., 2020); business students on presentation skills (McGovern et al., 2020); physics students with experiments (Pirker et al., 2020); and developing language skills or learning to present evidence to a jury (Hurrell & Baker, 2020). These studies have shown higher levels of student engagement and participation when learning in VR environments and some have even shown higher learning gains, particularly in the application of skills outside of the VR environment.

References

Hurrell, C., & Baker, J. (2020). Immersive learning: Applications of virtual reality for undergraduate education. College & Undergraduate Libraries, ahead-of-print(ahead-of-print), 1–13. https://doi.org/10.1080/10691316.2020.1796879

Labovitz, J., & Hubbard, C. (2020). The use of virtual reality in podiatric medical education. *Clinics in Podiatric Medicine and Surgery*, 37(2), 409-420.

McGovern, E., Moreira, G., & Luna-Nevarez, C. (2020). An application of virtual reality in education: Can this technology enhance the quality of students' learning experience? *Journal of Education for Business*, 95(7), 490-496.

Pirker, J., Holly, M., & Gütl, C. (2020, June). *Room scale virtual reality physics education: Use cases for the classroom.* In 2020 6th International Conference of the Immersive Learning Research Network (iLRN) (pp. 242-246). IEEE.

Sattar, M., Palaniappan, S., Lokman, A., Shah, N., Khalid, U., & Hasan, R. (2020). Motivating medical students using virtual reality based education. *International Journal of Emerging Technologies in Learning* (iJET), 15(2), 160-174.

19. Augmented Reality

Learning Objectives

- Differentiate between VR and AR
- Explore AR apps for use in education

Augmented reality (AR) is less immersive than virtual reality. Using a mobile device, AR makes use of apps to overlay reality with a virtual environment. *Pokemon Go!* is the best example of AR in recent years. AR tends to be a more affordable and manageable method of integrating technology in education and training over virtual reality because of the lack of external devices needed other than a mobile device. Apps such as *Anatomy 4D* and *Star Chart* use specific targets (printed paper targets and constellations, respectively) to determine which overlay to show the user. The user can then interact with the superimposed overlay and manipulate the virtual environment, as seen in Figure 12 where a museum patron uses an AR app to view detailed information on a painting.

Figure 12: Augmented reality at Museu de Mataró. Kippelboy. (Photographer). (2012, April 12). *Augmented reality at Museu de Mataró linking to Catalan Wikipedia articles.* [digital image]. https://commons.wikimedia.org/wiki/File:Augmented_reality_at_Museu_de_Matar%C3%B3_linking_to_Catalan_Wikipedia_(25).JPG

Augmented reality has been used with success in secondary school settings. There is a noticeable lack of empirical AR studies in higher education. AR has been used to engage and motivate secondary students in Earth Science (Sahin & Yimaz, 2020); to assist individuals with special needs learn life skills, social skills, motor skills, and learning skills (Baragash et al., 2020); and to teach students about anatomy and physiology (Chytas et al., 2020).

References

Baragash, R. S., Al-Samarraie, H., Alzahrani, A. I., & Alfarraj, O. (2020). Augmented reality in special education: A meta-analysis of single-subject design studies. *European Journal of Special Needs Education*, 35(3), 382-397.

Chytas, D., Johnson, E., Piagkou, M., Mazarakis, A., Babis, G., Chronopoulos, E., Nikolaou, V., Lazaridis, N., & Natsis, K. (2020). The role of augmented reality in anatomical education: An overview.

Annals of Anatomy, 229, 151463–151463. https://doi.org/10.1016/j.aanat.2020.151463

Sahin, D., & Yilmaz, R. M. (2020). The effect of augmented reality technology on middle school students' achievements and attitudes towards science education. *Computers & Education*, 144, 103710.

PART VI

CHAPTER 6 - FACULTY SHOWCASE

20. A game of Li[Fe] and Escape Rooms in an Integrated Engineering program

21. An Investor-Entrepreneur Simulation Game for Business Students

22. Nomenclature Card Games for Chemistry

PART VII

CHAPTER 7 - SUGGESTED ASSIGNMENTS

23. Gamer Profile Assignment

In order for us to implement any kind of Game-Based Learning, we need to understand what types of learners this strategy would appeal to. We need to understand gamers.

I would like you to prepare a case study of a gamer (not yourself) describing their habits, preferred games, style of play, preferences, and reflections on their own learning. This person can be someone who plays board games, card games, digital games, or mobile application games. This person can be of any age.

This case study can take many forms (video, online interactive, photo essay) but it cannot be a paper or PowerPoint. Think about the Bartle's Test – where do you think this person would fall?

For most students, this takes the form of a video profile approximately 5 minutes in length. In planning your project, you should both think about what you want to show and how you will show it. Some of this might be through narration, asking questions, through video of the player, or screencast of what they are doing. But also think about how you present this to tell a story and make a point. Can you show why this person chooses certain games? What makes it compelling? What have they learned from the game? How does it make them feel? Is there a social component to their play and learning?

You are essentially amateur field anthropologists—you should be trying to document the player's practices, motivations, and what they might be learning through the game. Make an effort not to judge or influence your subject; only observe and understand.

24. Needs / Gap Analysis

For this assignment, you will take a look at your own organization or an organization with which you are familiar. Conduct an informal, brief needs analysis that may require a learning or training intervention. Will adaptive or game-based learning be feasible options for this context? Why or why not? In your needs analysis, include:

- An analysis of your learners (age, education, language abilities) (Would these learners be able to perform if instruction used these techniques?).
- An analysis of current training/teaching practices (Do these techniques fit in with the teaching and learning culture? Would trainers/instructors be open to trying either technique?).
- An analysis of current technology tool availability (is there something available you could use to implement either technique?).
- An analysis of the current budget situation (Is there money to buy software or equipment, to pay designers?).
- A recommendation and rationale for or against adopting one or both Game-based Learning and Adaptive Learning.

You may want to use the checklist at http://www.hr-guide.com/Training/Checklist.htm to help you identify areas to consider.

25. Mini Adaptive Learning Plan

Create a mini-adaptive learning artifact or plan (i.e., a branching logic flow chart) and an implementation plan for its use.

Think about an opportunity you have either in your own organization or in a teaching and learning context with which you are familiar. Identify one learning goal that could be supported through the use of an adaptive learning solution. Design a mini-adaptive learning artifact or plan using the tool of your choice. You can either 1. fully design the artifact (e.g., a choose-your-own-adventure using google forms), OR 2. you can design a plan for an adaptive learning module. This would consist of laying out the branching logic and if/then items for the learning path.

Once your artifact or plan is drafted, develop a 1-2 page implementation plan for this learning experience. Include the following information in the implementation plan:

- Title of the learning experience where this artifact will be used.
- How the facilitators will be trained to use this artifact.
- Stakeholders and approvals needed to move forward with implementation.
- Any planning or testing stages that artifact implementation must go through.
- A timeline for implementation.

26. Commercial Product Analysis

Present an analysis of at least 5 currently available commercial adaptive or game-based learning solutions (video games, simulations, board games) that indicate suitability for a teaching and learning context with which you are familiar. This analysis should include a Graphic Organizer that details a comparison of commercial products. In your analysis, discuss whether the game or simulation provides the following learning elements:

- Literacy
- Communication
- Teamwork
- Problem-solving
- Forecasting
- Strategic thinking

27. Case Study Creation - Group Assignment

In order to identify and analyze organizational opportunities for the adoption of game-based or adaptive learning to achieve instructional outcomes, your group is going to develop a case study that describes an ideal GBL or adaptive learning adoption scenario.

Part 1

With your group, you will create one learning scenario where one of the following four strategies would be applicable as a learning technique: adaptive learning, gamification, games, simulations. You will not suggest which one of the four will apply, you will simply describe the learning context. The entire case study can be fictional if you choose. Include the following information in your case study:

- Organization
- Description of learners (age range, education level, technology experience)
- Learning need / Title of class
- Detailed description of the course or learning context
- List of technologies available (LMS, computer resources, etc.)
- Scope of learning context (how much time will be dedicated-one hour, one day a week, a semester)
- Any other details the group thinks would be relevant for choosing a strategy

Part 2

In 1-3 paragraphs, create a brief learning strategy using games, simulations, adaptive learning, or gamification. In one synthesized discussion, describe which strategy your group chose, why it is best suited for that case, and give us an overview of your group's vision for implementation.

Part 3

Group Case Study Response: As a group, choose 1 case study to review. With your group, create a learning strategy using games, simulations, adaptive learning, or gamification. In one synthesized discussion post, describe which strategy your group chose, why it is best suited for that case, and give us an overview of your group's vision for implementation.

28. Design an original game, simulation, or adaptive learning scenario

Kurt Squire describes endogenous games as games whose contexts and design are closely intertwined, as opposed to exogenous games, which serve as empty receptacles for bits of knowledge. We are all familiar with exogenous games. They are the trivia-type games that are popular on TV and in classrooms. They are popular in classrooms because they are easy to design and implement. However, they do not represent "good" games in the sense that they do not represent a meaningful ideological world.

Working individually, you will have the opportunity to design an original game, simulation, or adaptive learning scenario. Please note that *designing* is not the same as developing or implementing the game or simulation. Even though we are designing board or digital/video games and simulations, you do not have to create a digital game or simulation if that is the option you choose.

Your **game, simulation, or adaptive learning proposal** must contain the following elements:

1. Title
2. Overview (200 words)
3. Learning goals & educational theory (500 words)
4. Research: a report on other similar games, simulations, or adaptive learning studies that informed your decision (500 words)
5. Rules: the rules of your game, simulation, or adaptive learning scenario
6. Interface & artwork: to make your proposal more powerful, you

should include sketches of key screens and interactions, you may (optionally) include drafts of designs and other artwork that contribute to the game or simulation aesthetics

{*Instructors: This can be an iterative writing process. For example:*

In Week 7, you will turn in a (very) rough draft to receive peer feedback. In Week 8, you will give your peers your feedback. In Week 9, you will turn in the final draft of your assignment. You will also include the feedback you provided to your peers on their projects with your final draft so be sure to save them in a Word document.}

Example Simulation Design

Example Game Design

29. Instructional Plan

For this assignment, you will design and create an instructional plan that includes the following components: goals, objectives, GBL or adaptive learning instructional strategies, learning activities, details for implementation, and an evaluation plan.

Think of a course or training session you would likely be responsible for planning for your workplace or for a workplace with which you are familiar. This can be any type of learning experience (workplace training, a college-level course, a community education project, Bible study, book club workshop, conference workshop, etc.)

Create a deliverable that includes all of the following elements regarding your course or training session:

- The specific name and title of the course or training session
- A description and purpose of the selected course or training session
- The target audience: conduct an audience analysis and then describe the characteristics of the target audience
- Length of course or training session
- 2 to 4 goals for your course or training session based on your course or training session description
- 1 to 3 learning objectives that align with each of your stated goals
- Descriptions of game-based or adaptive learning instructional strategies and activities you will use in the course or training session
- Resources needed and materials that must be prepared
- Total length of time your course or training will take
- Individuals involved (facilitator, learners, administrators) with implementation

- Details of how your plan will be implemented
- How you will know participants are learning during the session. What formative assessments will you use?
- How you will evaluate the effectiveness of the training or learning experience.

Index